Original title:

Heart to Heart: Strengthening Intimacy

Author: Eliora Lumiste

ISBN HARDBACK: 978-9916-89-067-7

ISBN PAPERBACK: 978-9916-89-068-4

ISBN EBOOK: 978-9916-89-069-1

Beneath the Surface

In shadows deep, the secrets lie,
Whispers soft, as currents sigh.
Bubbles rise from depths unknown,
Life unfolds, the truth is shown.

Hidden worlds in colors bright,
Silent dances in the night.
Allies form in silent trust,
Nature's art of joy and rust.

Each wave tells a tale to tell,
Echoes from a distant swell.
A canvas drawn with water's hand,
A fleeting glimpse of spirits' band.

Calm surfaces can hide despair,
Floating dreams in salty air.
Yet beneath, a heartbeat throbs,
Life persists, through ebbs and mobs.

A realm untouched by human strife,
Beneath the surface, pulses life.
In unity, we find our place,
Eternal rhythm, timeless grace.

Constellations of Connection

Stars align in darkened skies,
Guiding sailors, distant cries.
A web of lights, a cosmic dance,
Intertwined, our fates romance.

Each twinkle holds a story dear,
Of whispered hopes, dreams drawing near.
Across the void, the sparks unite,
Illuminating paths of light.

In vastness, we seek our kin,
In the silent night, we begin.
Threads of gold weave through our hearts,
A tapestry where love imparts.

Celestial maps chart our way,
Through storms of doubt, in bright array.
We navigate with gentle grace,
Finding home in each other's space.

Beneath the glow, connections bloom,
A constellation in the gloom.
In every heartbeat, every breath,
We trace the lines that conquer death.

Dance of the Unseen

In shadows cast by flickering lights,
The unseen dance on silent nights.
Footfalls echo in whispered air,
A presence felt, though never there.

Curtains sway with unseen grace,
Time slows down in this sacred space.
Each turn, each spin, a tale unfolds,
In the dark, the spirit molds.

Hands that lift, though not in sight,
Moving freely, wild with delight.
The music plays, a gentle tease,
In the hush, our souls find ease.

Gravity bends to will and whim,
As shadows twist and lights grow dim.
The dance of life, both fierce and sweet,
In every pulse, we feel the beat.

With every breath, a story told,
In rhythms soft and brazen bold.
We celebrate what can't be seen,
In our hearts, the sacred sheen.

Silent Conversations

In glances shared, our voices meet,
A language soft, both pure and sweet.
Words unspoken, yet so clear,
In silence, we draw each other near.

The touch of hands, a tender sign,
Connection forged in spaces fine.
Understanding flows like gentle streams,
In quietude, we share our dreams.

Eyes reveal what lips can't say,
In every pause, the heart's ballet.
Listening close to the pulse of time,
In murmurs soft, our spirits climb.

A breath is worth a thousand years,
In silent joy, we shed our fears.
With every heartbeat, a promise lies,
In silence, love forever flies.

So let us linger in this hush,
Where hearts collide without a rush.
In every moment, let us find,
A world of meaning, intertwined.

Where Stories Intertwine

In the garden where tales bloom,
Whispers dance through the air,
Echoes of laughter take flight,
History woven with care.

Pages turn, hearts unite,
Lost in the glow of the night,
Every word holds a spark,
Painting dreams in the dark.

Paths crossed in a fleeting glance,
Moments captured in a trance,
With every twist, fate aligns,
In the book where love shines.

Threads of fate, gently sewn,
Stories shared, never alone,
Under the stars, secrets gleam,
Life unfolds like a dream.

Together, we write our own tale,
Every heartbeat, a fresh sail,
In the spaces where we reside,
Where stories and souls collide.

Kindred Spirits Alight

Two souls dancing in the breeze,
In a world where time stands still,
Moments shared beneath the trees,
Hearts intertwined with goodwill.

Laughter echoes through the night,
Underneath the silver moon,
In your eyes, the world feels right,
Every heartbeat, a sweet tune.

Kindred spirits, side by side,
In silence, a thousand words,
In the warmth, our worries hide,
With each glance, love's song is heard.

Through the storms, we'll find our way,
Hand in hand, never apart,
In the light of a brand-new day,
You forever hold my heart.

With every dawn, new dreams arise,
Together, we'll reach the skies,
In the fire of our delight,
Kindred spirits shining bright.

Unraveled Threads of Love

In the tapestry of days gone by,
Threads of love weave in and out,
Every moment, a gentle sigh,
In this weave, of joy and doubt.

Knots of fear try to ensnare,
But in your arms, I'm always found,
Through the chaos, we repair,
Unraveled threads that are profound.

With each heartbeat, we redefine,
Every stitch, a tale untold,
In the fabric, you are mine,
With warmth that weaves through the cold.

Together we mend, together we grow,
Through the seasons, hand in hand,
In this love, we let it show,
Unraveled threads, forever stand.

Through the years, this truth we find,
In each other, solace and grace,
Through every tear, love is blind,
In our hearts, we hold our place.

Tapestry of Two

In a world of colors bright,
We weave stories with our lives,
Threads of laughter, threads of light,
In the fabric, love survives.

Each moment a stitch so dear,
Patterns changing, yet so true,
In your gaze, I find no fear,
In this tapestry of two.

With every sigh, each gentle touch,
Our journey flows like a stream,
In the quiet, love speaks much,
Together, we live the dream.

Through the storms and gentle calm,
We create a vivid art,
In the weave, your soothing balm,
Binding together heart to heart.

With each sunset, colors blend,
In the twilight's soft embrace,
In our hearts, dreams never end,
Tapestry of love's sweet grace.

Unspoken Promises

In the silence where words fade,
Hearts whisper the vows made.
Promises linger in the air,
Untouched by doubt, stripped bare.

Every glance holds a story,
In shadows, we find glory.
Secrets dance behind closed eyes,
In the depths, the truth lies.

Hope trembles on the tongue,
While our song remains unsung.
The future waits, patiently still,
Unraveling with quiet will.

In the night, we softly tread,
With dreams that remain unread.
Each heartbeat a shared refrain,
Binding us through joy and pain.

With every sigh, unspoken grace,
In this moment, we find our place.
Between the chaos and the calm,
Beneath it all, a soothing balm.

A Layered Embrace

In the warmth of a soft cocoon,
We drift beneath a silver moon.
Gentle whispers float through air,
In this haven, free from care.

Fingers trace the lines we draw,
Feeling love without a flaw.
Entwined bodies, so divine,
Lost within your heart and mine.

Each moment a fragile thread,
Stitched with words once left unsaid.
In silence, our spirits rise,
Exploring depths, beyond the skies.

Layers peel with every sigh,
Revealing dreams that never die.
Wrapped in hopes, we remain whole,
As time weaves through our souls.

In the dance of shadows cast,
We find a love that holds us fast.
In this layered, sweet embrace,
Together we have found our place.

The Light We Share

In twilight's glow, our eyes collide,
Two hearts beating side by side.
Stars twinkle in a velvet sky,
Illuminating dreams that fly.

Each word spoken like a spark,
Kindling warmth within the dark.
We gather hope, like summer rain,
Nourishing love, easing pain.

With every dawn, our spirits rise,
Chasing shadows, breaking ties.
In laughter's light, we bloom anew,
Reflecting all that we pursue.

Through storms, we find our steady ground,
In each heartbeat, love resounds.
Hand in hand, we journey far,
Guided by our brightest star.

Together, we create a flame,
Kindling memories without shame.
In the warmth, we find our grace,
In the light, we share our space.

Interwoven Souls

In the tapestry of fate, we weave,
Threads of love that won't deceive.
Every moment stitched with care,
Destined hearts beyond compare.

In the fabric of the night,
Our spirits dance, a wondrous sight.
With every touch, we take our flight,
Soaring high, hearts burning bright.

The world fades in our embrace,
Finding solace in this place.
Together, connected as one,
Harmony in the setting sun.

Through the trials, we shall stand,
Forever linked, hand in hand.
The patterns shift but never break,
In each challenge, love we make.

Interwoven, our souls entwined,
A bond that's timeless, undefined.
In this dance, we lose control,
Embracing the rhythm of our soul.

Melding Dreams

In quiet nights where shadows play,
Our dreams entwine, begin to sway.
Stars whisper softly, secrets shared,
In the tapestry, we once dared.

Crimson skies embrace the dawn,
Hope arises where love is drawn.
Each vision built on whispered sighs,
Melding dreams as daylight dies.

Through the fog, we find our way,
Catching light, we choose to stay.
Hand in hand, we face the stars,
No longer sailing on our scars.

Time unfolds in gentle grace,
Lost in moments, we find our place.
Heartbeats echo, a rhythm true,
Melding dreams that dance for two.

With every breath, a promise made,
In this quiet, we won't fade.
A world inspired, all our own,
In melding dreams, we have grown.

The Language of Touch

Fingers trace the lines of fate,
In tender moments, hearts palpitate.
A brush, a nudge, a silent call,
In the language of touch, we share it all.

Whispers linger in the air,
The warmth of skin, a loving care.
Eyes will sparkle, sparks ignite,
In this dance of shadows and light.

Emotions rise, a gentle tide,
In the silent places, we can't hide.
Every caress a story told,
In the language of touch, love unfolds.

Locking gazes, a world so vast,
In a heartbeat, we hold the past.
An embrace that muffles the noise,
In the language of touch, we find our joys.

With every movement, connections weave,
A tapestry only we conceive.
So speak to me without a word,
In the language of touch, our hearts are stirred.

A Canvas of Us

Beneath the hues of twilight's glow,
We paint our story, line by line, slow.
Colors blend in a vibrant swirl,
On a canvas where dreams unfurl.

Every stroke a moment caught,
Whispers of love in every thought.
In vivid shades, we express our fears,
A canvas of us through laughter and tears.

Blues of sorrow, pinks of cheer,
Every color tells us we are near.
From shadows stark to light's embrace,
Our masterpiece finds its own pace.

Golden sunrises brush the sky,
In the heart's art, we learn to fly.
With every hue, our spirits rise,
In a canvas of us, love never lies.

So let the world fade from view,
In this sanctuary, just us two.
A palette rich, a love so vast,
On a canvas of us, our hearts are cast.

Breath of Understanding

In the silence where we dwell,
There exists a truth we know so well.
Gentle moments, softly shared,
In the breath of understanding, hearts laid bare.

Words may falter, meanings shift,
Yet in this closeness, we find our gift.
With every sigh and every glance,
We weave the threads of our lasting dance.

Through storms that may come, we'll stand tall,
With roots dug deep, we will not fall.
The rhythm of souls, a sweet refrain,
In the breath of understanding, love will remain.

Time may test, but bonds hold tight,
Illuminating the darkest night.
In shared silence, a world we create,
In the breath of understanding, we elevate.

So let our spirits intertwine,
With every heartbeat, divine design.
In this essence, we find the key,
In the breath of understanding, we are free.

The Symphony of Us

In harmony we blend our hearts,
With every note, the magic starts.
Together we create a song,
A melody where we belong.

Through every storm, we find our way,
Our voices joined, a warm display.
With laughter echoing through the night,
In love's embrace, we find the light.

In gentle whispers, secrets shared,
Each moment shows how much we cared.
The symphony, a dance divine,
In perfect time, your heart is mine.

As seasons change, the music swells,
In every chord, a story tells.
The rhythm of our lives so true,
Forever played, just me and you.

With every breath, a sweet refrain,
In joy and sorrow, love's our gain.
Together we will face the test,
In this symphony, we are blessed.

Anchors of Love

In troubled seas, our hearts entwine,
You are my anchor, pure and fine.
Through raging storms, we hold the tie,
With love as deep as oceans high.

The tides may rise, the winds may roar,
Yet in your arms, I fear no more.
Your steady gaze, my guiding star,
Together, love, we've come so far.

Roots of trust in fertile ground,
In every silence, peace is found.
We'll weather all, come what may,
With anchors strong, we'll find our way.

In evening's calm, we drift and dream,
Two souls united, a sacred theme.
With every heartbeat, time will show,
The depth of love we both will know.

In life's embrace, let's forge our fate,
In love's sweet arms, we celebrate.
With every trial, we rise above,
Together always, anchors of love.

A Mosaic of Souls

In colors bright, our spirits blend,
Each piece reflects a warmth we send.
A tapestry of dreams takes flight,
In every shard, a spark of light.

We gather moments, hand in hand,
In laughter shared, we make our stand.
With every heartbeat, stories told,
Our mosaic shines with hues of gold.

Through trials faced and joys embraced,
Together, time cannot erase.
A patchwork rich, of love and grace,
In unity, we find our place.

Each fragment tells of where we've been,
In every smile, the strength within.
The art of living, bright and true,
In every piece, I'm lost in you.

As life unfolds, our masterpiece,
In every bond, our love's release.
A mosaic crafted from our souls,
Together, we make each other whole.

Finding Joy in Togetherness

In quiet moments, laughter blooms,
Together shared, we chase our glooms.
In every glance, a spark ignites,
Finding joy in our shared sights.

With open hearts, we walk this road,
Each step we take, our love bestowed.
Through ups and downs, we hold on tight,
In every challenge, we find light.

With hands entwined, we face the day,
In your embrace, worries drift away.
Every memory, a treasure found,
In joyful whispers, love is crowned.

As stars align in evening's glow,
We find the paths we long to know.
In simple things, our hearts take flight,
Finding joy in the shared delight.

Let's paint our dreams across the sky,
With every laugh, our spirits high.
Together always, come what may,
In love's embrace, we find our way.

Unraveled Layers

Beneath my skin, a story hides,
Waves of time and tides abide.
Threads of joy, strands of sorrow,
Each layer whispers of tomorrow.

In the mirror, shadows play,
Unraveling truths from yesterday.
Moments stitched in fragile seams,
Telling tales of silent dreams.

Echoes linger, soft and clear,
Memories dance, drawing near.
Peeling back the ancient fears,
Finding solace through the years.

Every fold a secret's grace,
In this journey, find my place.
Hearts entwined, through thick and thin,
Layer by layer, where I begin.

Like petals fall, revealing light,
Unraveled layers, pure and bright.
Each story woven, rich and vast,
In the tapestry of our past.

In Step with One Another

Hand in hand, we walk the line,
Echoes blend, your heart with mine.
Footsteps find a rhythm sweet,
In step with one, our souls complete.

Through grassy fields and starlit skies,
Together we seek, always wise.
Side by side, both day and night,
In step with love, hearts taking flight.

Every laugh, a note in song,
In this dance, we both belong.
Twirls and spins, a gentle sway,
In step with dreams, come what may.

Across the valleys, mountains high,
With every breath, we touch the sky.
Together strong, we face the tide,
In step forever, side by side.

With every stumble, we learn and grow,
In this journey, our love will flow.
In step with one, forever true,
In this life, it's me and you.

Intwine me

Wrap your arms, a gentle bind,
In your warmth, solace I find.
Twisting paths that lead us near,
Intwine me close, erase the fear.

Fingers thread through strands of fate,
In your hold, my heart won't wait.
Laughter echoes, love's embrace,
Intwine me here, in this sacred space.

Whispers soft, like summer rain,
In your touch, I feel no pain.
Knot my spirit to your song,
Intwine me deep, where we belong.

Every heartbeat, rhythms play,
Interwoven, night and day.
In your gaze, I lose my way,
Intwine me near, let love stay.

In this dance, beneath the stars,
Time stands still, erasing scars.
With every breath, let passions free,
Intwine me now, eternally.

Under the Same Moon

Beneath the sky where shadows creep,
Under the same moon, secrets keep.
Whispers carried on the breeze,
Uniting hearts, bringing ease.

In silver glow, our dreams align,
Paths converge, your soul with mine.
Every twinkle, fate's design,
Under the same moon, we intertwine.

Stories told in quiet light,
Finding warmth in the night.
Through the darkness, we will roam,
Under the same moon, we find home.

Distant stars, as guides they shine,
In this moment, love divine.
Holding tight with hearts so bold,
Under the same moon, tales unfold.

With every rise, a new embrace,
Together we will find our place.
Under the moon, forever true,
In this dance, it's me and you.

Intimate Murmurs

In the silence of the night,
Soft whispers paint the air,
Between heartbeats, secrets flow,
Two souls dancing without a care.

The moonlight bathes our dreams,
Casting shadows on our past,
In these moments, we confide,
A bond that's meant to last.

With every touch, a story told,
Glimmers of a deeper truth,
In the warmth of your embrace,
I find the spark of youth.

Time fades away in your gaze,
Infinite worlds reside within,
In the quiet, we explore,
Where love and trust begin.

Intimate whispers linger on,
Echoes of the night's sweet song,
In this sacred space we share,
Together, we know we belong.

Waves of Understanding

Tides rise and fall with grace,
In the dance of ebb and flow,
With every rise, new thoughts emerge,
In the depths, truths beautifully grow.

Waves crash upon the sandy shore,
Each one telling stories deep,
In their rhythm, we find peace,
And hear the promises they keep.

The ocean speaks in murmured tones,
Carrying dreams upon its breast,
In the silence, a reassuring voice,
Whispers of our shared quest.

As currents pull us to the deep,
We learn to ride the stormy seas,
In this element, we are one,
Bound by the winds' gentle breeze.

With each wave, a new beginning,
In the tides of understanding near,
Together we journey, hand in hand,
Navigating what we hold dear.

Shelters of Solace

In the corners of my mind,
I find refuge from the storm,
Within these shelters, I feel safe,
Where the heart can stay warm.

Days may pass like fleeting shadows,
But inside, I hold my ground,
In these quiet, sacred spaces,
An inner peace is found.

Beneath the branches of an old tree,
I cradle all my hopes and fears,
In the gentle whisper of the leaves,
I hear the song of passing years.

Here I weave my dreams by night,
In a tapestry of stars,
Each thread a moment, brilliantly spun,
As I gaze upon their scars.

In these shelters, we are free,
To linger, love, and simply be,
Together, we create a home,
In solace, we find harmony.

The Art of Knowing

In the quiet of a glance,
Lies the depth of understanding,
A language crafted in silence,
Where hearts are ever expanding.

Every story etched in time,
We unravel like ancient scrolls,
With patience, we trace the lines,
Connecting fragmented souls.

The art of knowing, soft and wise,
Holds the power to unite,
In the spaces between our words,
We find our shared light.

Through laughter and through tears,
We learn to read each other's heart,
In this dance of souls entwined,
Together, we create art.

With every breath, a chance to see,
The beauty of what lies beneath,
In the art of knowing you,
I find my deepest wreath.

Threads of Connection

In the quiet moments we find,
A thread that binds, strong yet kind.
Through laughter shared and tears that flow,
In every heartbeat, love will grow.

Tangled paths, yet we align,
In whispered dreams, your hand in mine.
Together forged through storms we brave,
In the tapestry, our hearts engrave.

Each secret shared, a stitch so fine,
In this rich fabric, life divine.
We sew the joys, we mend the fray,
In every challenge, come what may.

Though shadows cast, we're not alone,
With every thread, a kindness shown.
The colors blend, your soul, my art,
In the tapestry, you fill my heart.

So let us weave, and never cease,
In this creation, we find our peace.
Through every year, let love connect,
A masterpiece in every aspect.

In the Space Between

In the silence that we share,
A world awakens, laid bare.
The breath we take, a gentle pause,
In the space, our hearts explore.

Words unspoken hold their weight,
In the hush, we contemplate.
Every glance, a story tells,
In the quiet, emotion swells.

What's not said is just as clear,
In that space, I feel you near.
A canvas blank, yet painted bright,
In the shadows, there's also light.

The moments linger, suspended time,
In the stillness, souls can climb.
An unbroken bond that we create,
In the silence, love resonates.

Through every heartbeat, we shall glide,
In that space, there's no need to hide.
So let us cherish what we find,
In the silence, our souls aligned.

Secrets Shared in Silence

In whispered tones, a bond we weave,
A silent pact, we both believe.
With eyes that speak, and hearts laid bare,
In the stillness, secrets share.

Each moment hides a tale untold,
In quiet spaces, we grow bold.
The warmth between us, softly spun,
In silent truths, we are as one.

No need for words when hearts converse,
In the hush, our souls immerse.
A language formed, both deep and wide,
In the silence, love can't hide.

Through every glance, a story comes,
In the quiet, the heart still drums.
For what is shared without a sound,
In the silence, trust is found.

So let us keep this sacred space,
In whispers soft, our love's embrace.
For secrets shared in silent grace,
Are treasures kept, time can't erase.

The Dance of Vulnerability

In the light of truth, we step and sway,
With bare souls open, come what may.
In every glance, a fragile plea,
In the dance of vulnerability.

With trembling hearts, we learn to trust,
To be seen whole, to feel the thrust.
As we twirl through joys and fears,
In this dance, we shed our tears.

The rhythm guides, we fall and rise,
In each misstep, a sweet disguise.
With every beat, we find our flow,
In vulnerability, we grow.

The space between, electric spark,
In silent moments, we leave a mark.
Together lost, yet never alone,
In vulnerability, love is shown.

So take my hand, let's dance once more,
In the open, we can soar.
For in this grace, the truth we see,
In vulnerability, we are free.

Intimate Tapestries

In the quiet moments shared,
Threads of whispers softly bared,
Stitched with laughter, love's sweet song,
A tapestry where we belong.

Fingers trace the woven past,
Hopes and dreams embraced so fast,
Patterns shift, yet heartbeats stay,
In this cloth, we find our way.

Colors blend and sometimes fade,
Yet the bond will never jade,
Every patch a story told,
In this fabric, hearts unfold.

With every knot, our spirits soar,
Intertwined forevermore,
Underneath the stars we lay,
In our tapestry, we play.

Woven whispers, night and day,
In this dance, we softly sway,
Close as shadows in moonlight,
Intimate tapestries ignite.

The Color of Us

In the spectrum where we meet,
Our hues blend, a soft heartbeat,
Crimson blush and azure skies,
In your gaze, my spirit flies.

Palette rich with dreams anew,
Every shade reflects what's true,
From the dawn to twilight's glow,
The color of us starts to flow.

Through the strokes of joy and pain,
We create our sweet refrain,
In the canvas, shadows dance,
Coloring life with every chance.

Vivid greens of hope arise,
Underneath the painted skies,
Every moment's hue persists,
In the blend, our love exists.

The color of us, bold and bright,
Crafted in the soft moonlight,
A masterpiece, forever just,
In each other, we find trust.

Rituals of Togetherness

In the morning's gentle light,
We gather close, hearts in flight,
A simple touch, a knowing smile,
Rituals that stretch each mile.

With every laugh, the day's begun,
Together, we become as one,
Shared secrets over coffee's steam,
A sacred bond, a cherished dream.

Evenings wrap us in their glow,
Stories shared, the fire's flow,
In the twilight, whispers blend,
Rituals of love, they never end.

Hands entwined, we dance around,
In this circle, peace is found,
Every heartbeat, every sigh,
Strengthened bonds as years go by.

With the moon, we find our grace,
In these moments, we embrace,
Rituals of togetherness,
In unity, our hearts confess.

Pathways of Affection

Each step we take, a path is drawn,
In your light, my fears are gone,
With every turn, love's journey unfolds,
Pathways of affection, ours to hold.

Through winding roads of sun and shade,
In every moment, love's cascade,
Hand in hand, the world feels right,
Guided by the soft moonlight.

Over hills and valleys wide,
With you there, I feel alive,
Every pathway leads us near,
In each other, we persevere.

Through storms and sunny days we roam,
In your heart, I've found my home,
Side by side, we're never low,
Pathways of affection grow.

With laughter echoing in the air,
Journeying without a care,
In love's embrace, we find our way,
Together in life's grand ballet.

The Space Between Us

In shadows cast by moonlight's glow,
A silence lingers, soft and low.
We drift like ships on distant seas,
Yet feel the pull of memories.

Each breath a whisper, lost in air,
An unspoken bond we both share.
Though miles may stretch and nights grow long,
In heart's deep chamber, we belong.

The years may fade like autumn leaves,
Yet in the quiet, love believes.
A thread unseen, it tightly binds,
Across the distance, hearts aligned.

In the stillness, I hear your call,
A gentle echo through the hall.
It's more than space, it's where we dance,
In every moment, chance after chance.

So here we stand, in twilight's hue,
Not lost in space, but found in you.
For in the distance, love can see,
The sacred space that sets us free.

Embracing Vulnerability

Like petals soft, we start to bloom,
In honesty, we shed the gloom.
Each fear unveiled, a tender grace,
In every heart, a hidden place.

To bare the soul, it takes great trust,
In fragile moments, we adjust.
For in the cracks, the light pours in,
A beautiful dance where we begin.

With open arms, we face the storm,
In shared affection, we transform.
The courage found in showing scars,
Unites us gently, like the stars.

So let us speak, our truths unfold,
In warmth and kindness, hearts consoled.
For in this space where we confide,
Vulnerability's the truest guide.

Together strong, we rise and soar,
With every story, we explore.
For in the depths of what we share,
We find the strength to truly care.

Bridges of Trust

Upon the river of our dreams,
We build our bridges, so it seems.
With each plank laid, a promise made,
In the light of love, we won't fade.

The currents may twist, the winds may blow,
Yet hand in hand, we bravely go.
With patience strong and hearts so true,
Our sturdy bridge will see us through.

In laughter's echo, we find our path,
In loyalty's glow, escape the wrath.
A gentle touch, a knowing glance,
Constructs the space for our romance.

So let us walk this bridge we've built,
With tender words and no guilt.
In every step, we find our way,
Together strong, come what may.

For trust, my love, sets us apart,
A cornerstone of every heart.
Through trials faced and storms we must,
We grow together, bridge of trust.

In the Softest Moments

In twilight's hush, when shadows fall,
We find the magic in it all.
A gentle sigh, a warm embrace,
In quietude, we find our place.

The world outside may spin and race,
Yet here, it's just our secret space.
With whispered words and softest touch,
In these moments, we mean so much.

Like fading stars that light the night,
Your presence fills my heart with light.
In stillness shared, we breathe as one,
In every heartbeat, love's sweet song.

With every glance, a silent vow,
To cherish all, to live a now.
For in these softest moments dear,
We weave together, year by year.

So let the world keep on its pace,
We'll carve our niche, our sacred place.
For in the silence, love's refrain,
Echoes softly, again, again.

The Alchemy of Us

In twilight's glow, our shadows dance,
Two souls entwined in a fleeting chance.
Words like whispers, soft and sweet,
We blend the world beneath our feet.

A spark ignites, our hearts ignite,
Transforming silence into light.
With every laugh, we share our gold,
In this embrace, we break the mold.

We coil like vines around the truth,
Our dreams alive, eternal youth.
In the cauldron of our trust,
Magic brews in the breath of must.

Time fades slow, like honey's flow,
In every heartbeat, love will grow.
We are the art that fate designed,
In the alchemy of hearts entwined.

With every glance, we forge our fate,
Creating moments that resonate.
In this wonder, forever we're free,
The alchemy of you and me.

Mapping Our Souls

Through uncharted lands, we find our way,
With every tear, and every sway.
You draw the lines, I follow near,
Together mapping love sincere.

In the stars, our paths align,
With ink of fate, our dreams define.
Each heartbeat's echo, a guiding star,
In the silence, we travel far.

With open eyes, we tread the night,
Charting constellations in soft light.
In this adventure, side by side,
We've written volumes, in love we abide.

Each secret shared, a treasure found,
In this vast world, where dreams abound.
Together we'll write our story bold,
Mapping our souls, a love untold.

With every step, we'll paint the skies,
In vibrant colors of our sighs.
In this journey, we become whole,
As we navigate, mapping our souls.

Safe in Your Reflection

In mirrored depths, I see my heart,
The way you shine, a work of art.
In your reflection, I find my peace,
A sanctuary where fears cease.

Your laughter echoes, a sweet refrain,
In your embrace, there's no more pain.
With every glance, I feel the grace,
In your reflection, I find my place.

Through stormy nights and sunlit days,
You are the light in myriad ways.
In shadows cast, I seek your glow,
Safe in your reflection, love will grow.

I wander lost, yet find my home,
In mirrored worlds, I'm not alone.
Together here, our spirits rise,
As we reflect the boundless skies.

So let me linger, forever true,
In your reflection, just me and you.
In every moment, endlessly blessed,
Safe in your love, I find my rest.

Our Sanctuary of Secrets

In quiet corners, love's whispers dwell,
Our sanctuary, where stories swell.
With fragile hands, we weave the night,
Creating dreams within our sight.

Each secret held, a precious thread,
Binding our hearts where angels tread.
In the shadows, our laughter rings,
In this haven, our spirit sings.

The world outside can fade away,
In this refuge, forever we'll stay.
With every sigh, a story springs,
In the tapestry our love brings.

Through spoken vows and silent sighs,
We build our fortress 'neath the skies.
In shared glances, a knowing glance,
Our sanctuary, a treasured dance.

So here we'll dwell, in whispers sweet,
In every heartbeat, love's pulse beats.
This sanctuary, a sacred nest,
In our secrets, we find our rest.

Rhythm of Our Souls

In silence, hearts align,
A dance beneath the stars,
Our whispers fill the night,
Echoes from afar.

Each heartbeat sings a song,
A melody divine,
With every step we take,
Our spirits intertwine.

The moonlight casts a glow,
On paths we've yet to tread,
With every breath we share,
New dreams are gently said.

In twilight's warm embrace,
We find the strength to soar,
Together hand in hand,
Forever we explore.

The rhythm of our souls,
In harmony they stride,
With love as our guide,
We dance, we bide our time.

Nurturing the Unseen

In shadows where we dwell,
A tenderness unseen,
We plant our hopes and dreams,
In soil, rich and green.

With gentle hands we tend,
To seeds that yearn to grow,
In the quiet of the night,
Their strength begins to show.

Roots spread beneath the earth,
Drawing life from the deep,
Each moment, every breath,
A promise we will keep.

In the garden of the mind,
We nurture love and care,
For what is yet to bloom,
Is the beauty we will share.

The unseen, now revealed,
With colors bold and bright,
We celebrate the growth,
In the warmth of love's light.

The Poetry of Togetherness

In every shared glance,
A story starts to weave,
The poetry we write,
Is what we both believe.

Each laughter, every tear,
A verse upon the page,
In moments, fleeting swift,
We capture time and age.

With hands entwined in trust,
We pen our heartfelt lines,
Our souls, a canvas bright,
Where love forever shines.

Through chapters yet unknown,
Together we will roam,
In the book of life we'll find,
That this, our cherished home.

The poetry of us,
In rhythm, dance, and song,
With every twist of fate,
Together we belong.

Gardens of Affection

In a garden lush and wide,
Where hearts can freely bloom,
We sow the seeds of love,
Dispersing joy and room.

With every gentle touch,
New petals start to grow,
In colors bright and warm,
Their fragrance starts to show.

We nurture all that's pure,
Through seasons thick and thin,
In the soil of our trust,
Together, we begin.

A tapestry of hues,
In sunlight, rain, and shade,
Each moment in this space,
An art that we've created.

In gardens of affection,
We find our spirits blend,
With every bloom we share,
Our love will never end.

Threads of Kindred Spirits

In the quiet dusk, we weave our tales,
With laughter stitched between each breath.
A tapestry of dreams unveils,
Bound together beyond time and death.

With every glance, the stories flow,
Entwined hearts dancing in the light.
Through whispered secrets, love will grow,
Guiding us softly through the night.

Miles may part, yet souls remain,
Connected by a golden thread.
In joy or sorrow, through sun or rain,
Our spirits soar where memories tread.

Through trials faced, we find our way,
With hands outstretched, we heal the pain.
Together forged, we shall not sway,
In the embrace of love's sweet chain.

We'll gather storms and chase the stars,
As kindred spirits, heart to heart.
No distance closed, no fate that bars,
In unity, we make our start.

Whispered Confessions

In the stillness, shadows play,
Secrets murmured, hearts exposed.
Underneath the moon's soft ray,
Bare souls speak, their truths disclosed.

Each shared glance, a silent vow,
Where fears dissolve like morning mist.
In soft tones, we wonder how,
Love's gentle light keeps us kissed.

As stars align, we find our voice,
In whispered truths that bind us tight.
Through every tear, we claim our choice,
To face the dark and greet the light.

With open hearts, we dive so deep,
Into the depths of all we feel.
These whispered dreams, our nightly keep,
Granting strength, a bond so real.

In shadows cast and twilight's glow,
We'll weave our hopes with every sigh.
For in these whispers, love will grow,
Forever in the starry sky.

Lock and Key

In a world of doors yet unturned,
Hearts hold secrets, they learn to hide.
Each locking gaze, a lesson earned,
With love's sweet key, they will abide.

A heart once closed, tenderly turned,
Awakens dreams that softly glow.
With every twist, the fire burned,
A treasure found, as passions flow.

In whispered nights and tender sighs,
The key finds solace in the lock.
With every heartbeat, love complies,
Creating magic with a knock.

Each moment shared, a place to hide,
Reflecting trust in every shard.
Together, in this bliss, we bide,
Unlocking dreams, though life is hard.

No longer chained, we rise to see,
The dawning of our destiny.
For every lock, there is a key,
With love to guide, we shall be free.

A Journey Within

Beneath the surface, whispers call,
A path of quiet thoughts unfolds.
Through winding roads, we rise and fall,
Revealing wisdom the soul beholds.

In sacred space, the heart aligns,
Exploring depths where shadows play.
Through every breath, the spirit shines,
Guiding us gently on our way.

Amidst the storm, we learn to find,
The strength to stand, the tears to shed.
Each step we take is intertwined,
With echoes of the words unsaid.

Embracing stillness, we discover,
The layers of the self we keep.
Through gentle winds, we're like a lover,
Awakened by the dreams we reap.

As journeys end, new paths begin,
With every choice, the heart's art draws.
In joy and pain, we rise, we spin,
A dance of life, a sacred cause.

Sculpting Our Bond

In clay, we mold our dreams,
Soft whispers of the night,
With every touch, it seems,
Our hearts find shared delight.

Through patience, we create,
A figure strong and true,
Each curve, each twist of fate,
Reflects the love in you.

Together hand in hand,
As passions start to blend,
We shape a lasting brand,
A bond that will not end.

With colors bold and bright,
We paint our story clear,
The shadows kissed by light,
In love, we persevere.

A masterpiece unfolds,
Each layer tells our tale,
Through days both hot and cold,
In unity, we sail.

Harmonizing Hearts

Two melodies align,
In rhythm, side by side,
Our voices intertwine,
Creating love's sweet tide.

Each note a gentle caress,
Soft symphonies we weave,
In harmony, we bless,
The dreams that we believe.

Through highs and through lows,
We dance a tender waltz,
Together, love still grows,
A tune that never halts.

With strings that hum with glee,
And echoes from the past,
We write our history,
A love that's meant to last.

In perfect sync we play,
Our hearts forever joined,
Through night and into day,
In harmony, we're coined.

Echoes of Our Laughter

In moments filled with glee,
We share the lightest jest,
Each laugh a melody,
That life has truly blessed.

Through silly little games,
And stories from the heart,
In echoes, love inflames,
Where joy becomes an art.

As daylight starts to fade,
Our laughter fills the air,
In memories we've made,
A treasure soft and rare.

Each giggle and each cheer,
A bond that time won't break,
Through laughter, we are near,
Our love, a sweet earthquake.

In echoes that won't fade,
We cherish what we share,
A tapestry displayed,
Of moments filled with care.

Map of Our Memories

In corners we have roamed,
With every step we take,
Each path so well-honed,
A journey we create.

With markers set in time,
We trace the lines so clear,
In laughter and in rhyme,
Our story grows each year.

From mountains high we've climbed,
To oceans deep and wide,
Each memory we've timed,
Is where our love resides.

With every twist and turn,
We gather what we find,
In sharing, our hearts burn,
A treasure intertwined.

Through maps both bold and vast,
Of memories we hold near,
Together, unsurpassed,
Our love will persevere.

The Core Connection

In the silence, hearts align,
Whispers echo, pure and fine.
A bond that time cannot erase,
In each moment, love's embrace.

Through shadows cast, we gently weave,
With shared breaths, we dare believe.
Roots entwined beneath the earth,
In every heartbeat, find our worth.

A glance, a touch, electric spark,
In the daylight, in the dark.
Together we can face the storm,
In our spirits, we are warm.

A canvas painted red and blue,
Each stroke tells tales both old and new.
In laughter's joy, in sorrow's sigh,
We build our dreams, you and I.

From depths unseen, we rise and soar,
With every challenge, wanting more.
Our core connection, strong and true,
In all we are, I cherish you.

Flames of Connection

In the night, a fire glows,
Warming hearts, as passion flows.
Each flicker tells a tale of old,
Of dreams and wishes yet untold.

We gather close, side by side,
In this warmth, our fears subside.
With every spark, our spirits dance,
In the glow, we find our chance.

Through the embers, visions flare,
Hope ignites in the crisp air.
In the blaze, our souls ignite,
Flames of connection burn so bright.

Moments shared in flickering light,
Building bridges through the night.
In our laughter, in our tears,
We find solace through the years.

As the fire dwindles low,
In its warmth, our love will grow.
Forever fueled by trust and grace,
In this connection, we find our place.

Tides of Trust

Waves crash softly on the shore,
In their rhythm, I find more.
With each tide, a promise true,
In every ebb, I stand with you.

The moon pulls gently, guiding hands,
Together, we draw in the sands.
In the depths, where secrets hide,
We cast our nets, love as our guide.

Rising high, then sinking low,
In this dance, our feelings flow.
Trust the tides, they'll never lie,
In their waves, our spirits fly.

When storms arise and waters churn,
In the chaos, we will learn.
For every surge, we stand as one,
Our bond, unbroken, never done.

As the seas reflect the sky,
In their depths, we learn to fly.
Tides of trust, a sacred grace,
In your arms, I find my place.

Moments Wrapped in Gold

In the dawn, soft light unfolds,
Every second, moments gold.
Time stands still, a captured glance,
In your presence, I find romance.

A gentle breeze whispers near,
Every heartbeat, crystal clear.
In tiny laughs, in shared delight,
We wrap our dreams in purest light.

Every sunset paints the skies,
In hues of hope, our spirits rise.
Wrapped in warmth, we hold on tight,
In love's embrace, we shine so bright.

From whispered dreams to joys we share,
Moments precious, beyond compare.
In the stillness, in the rush,
Life's sweet magic, in every hush.

Time may pass, but love will stay,
In every golden moment, play.
Wrapped in softness, hand in hand,
In this life, together we stand.

Ties That Bind

In shadows we find our way,
Through laughter and tears we stay.
A bond that won't easily fray,
Together, come what may.

Hands held tight in dark and light,
In silence, our hearts take flight.
The whispers that feel so right,
We shine like stars at night.

Through storms that may shake our ground,
In every heartbeat, love is found.
In the chaos, we are sound,
In each other, we are bound.

With every promise softly made,
In gentle trust, we are laid.
In every choice, unafraid,
Our connection won't fade.

So here we stand, side by side,
In this journey, our hearts guide.
In every moment, love's the tide,
Together, forever, we're tied.

Echoes of Togetherness

In the echoes of laughter shared,
In moments we crafted and bared.
In memories, our souls prepared,
A rhythm, deep and ensnared.

Through storms and sunlight, we roam,
In each other, a sweet home.
Wherever we wander and comb,
Together, we find our dome.

The whispers of dreams we chase,
In this timeless, sacred space.
With every heartbeat, we embrace,
In love's gentle, warm grace.

The distance between us may wane,
Yet, we dance in joy and pain.
With each step, love's refrain,
In togetherness, we remain.

So let the world fade away,
In this moment, we will stay.
Through every dawn, night, and day,
Echoes of love here to play.

Threads of Unspoken Promises

In the delicate threads we weave,
In silence, our hearts believe.
With every glance, we perceive,
A love that helps us achieve.

Through the moments left unsaid,
In dreams where our hearts are led.
Each promise in whispers spread,
A tapestry gently bred.

With hands intertwined so near,
In the warmth, we have no fear.
The future draws ever clear,
In our closeness, we adhere.

Unspoken vows in the air,
In a dance, both bold and rare.
We create our world, a pair,
In love's beauty, we declare.

So here's to the bonds we form,
In love's embrace, we are warm.
Through life's journey, we transform,
In every storm, we will swarm.

Intimacy in Bloom

In the garden of hearts that grow,
Where gentle winds of love blow.
Each petal's kiss, soft and slow,
In this sacred space, we know.

With the dawn, our spirits sing,
In unison, the joy we bring.
As blossoms dance in the spring,
In our souls, a magic ring.

The secrets whispered at night,
In the hush, our dreams take flight.
In every touch, pure delight,
Together, we are the light.

As we nurture what's inside,
In affection, we shall abide.
With every challenge, love's our guide,
In intimacy, time can't bide.

So let our love continue to bloom,
In each heartbeat, dispelling gloom.
In this place, we find our room,
Together, we shall consume.

Resonance of Silence

In the hush of night, whispers play,
Secrets linger, drift away.
Stars above, a quiet gleam,
In the dark, we softly dream.

Echoing thoughts in stillness found,
Heartbeats dance to a gentle sound.
Nature calls, a silent song,
In this peace, we all belong.

Moments pause, the world lies still,
In the silence, time we fill.
Cocooned in calm, we seek the light,
Resonances bloom, taking flight.

Words unspoken, eyes convey,
In the quiet, love will stay.
Here we find what words can't share,
In resonance, a bond so rare.

The Journey Within

Steps taken softly, paths unfold,
Within the heart, stories told.
Wandering thoughts, a treasure chest,
In silence, we seek our rest.

Layers peel, revealing soul,
In quietude, we become whole.
Every heartbeat a guiding star,
The journey leads us, near and far.

Reflections beckon, mirrors speak,
In vulnerability, we seek.
What lies beneath, we dare to know,
Through dark valleys, courage will grow.

Moments linger, echoes stay,
In solitude, we find our way.
The journey inward, bold and bright,
Illuminating our deepest light.

Tidal Waves of Togetherness

Waves crash gently on the shore,
Together bound, we seek for more.
In unity, our spirits rise,
A dance of hearts beneath the skies.

Holding hands, we feel the pull,
In this tide, emotions full.
Beneath the surface, currents blend,
In our hearts, love knows no end.

As storms may come, and winds may howl,
In each other, we find our growl.
Together strong, we'll navigate,
On waves of trust, we contemplate.

In every swell, connections weave,
Tidal forces, we believe.
Through ups and downs, we rise anew,
In the ocean of me and you.

Bound by Vulnerability

In open hearts, we find the key,
To share our truths, to simply be.
Each fragile whisper breaks the ice,
In vulnerability, we find our ties.

Unraveled fears, a sacred space,
In honesty, we embrace grace.
Letting go of what we hide,
In this trust, we dare to bide.

With every tear, a story flows,
In our depths, compassion grows.
Embracing flaws, we break the mold,
In vulnerability, we are bold.

Strength in softness, bonds entwined,
In shared scars, true love is lined.
Together we thrive, unmasked and free,
Bound by the beauty of you and me.

Unraveled Stories

In whispers of the night, they call,
Secrets woven, one and all.
Pages turned with trembling hands,
Dreams unspooled, like golden strands.

Faded photos in the light,
Echoes of forgotten plight.
Every tale, a gentle tear,
Woven beauty, ever near.

Voices linger in the breeze,
Tales of love, lost memories.
Silent shadows twirl and dance,
Life's grand story, given chance.

Threads of hope, in heart's embrace,
Unraveled time, a sacred space.
In each sorrow, joy we find,
Binding us, the ties that bind.

With every breath, the stories grow,
Written softly, in ebb and flow.
In the quiet, we discover,
Life's great book, our souls uncover.

Raindrops and Reflections

Raindrops cling to window panes,
Softly whispering nature's gains.
Puddles form, a mirrored dream,
Rippling with the silver gleam.

Clouds drift by in shades of gray,
Painting skies with shades that sway.
Each drop tells a tale anew,
Nature's song, forever true.

Children splash with gleeful cries,
Laughter dances, reaching skies.
Joy unbound, in each embrace,
Raindrops fall, a gentle grace.

As daylight fades, reflections glow,
In mirrored worlds, our thoughts flow.
In quiet moments, wisdom sought,
Life unfolds in every thought.

When storms subside, a calm remains,
Nature's heartbeat in its chains.
Raindrops hug the earth so tight,
Whispering dreams into the night.

Building Sanctuaries

With every brick, a story laid,
A sacred space where dreams are made.
Walls of love and laughter rise,
Underneath the vast, soft skies.

Windows open, hearts in view,
Sunlight streaming, warmth anew.
With each color, hope entwined,
In every corner, peace defined.

Plants and flowers grace the room,
Filling hearts, dispelling gloom.
With gentle hands, we craft, we mold,
A haven where our dreams unfold.

Gathered 'round in unity,
Voices blend in harmony.
In this space, we all belong,
Building dreams, a vibrant song.

With open doors, we greet the night,
Together, guiding through the fright.
Building sanctuaries, side by side,
In warmth and love, our hearts abide.

Heartbeats in Sync

In twilight's glow, our pulses race,
Two souls captured in this space.
Silent echoes, rhythms blend,
In every heartbeat, love transcends.

With gentle whispers, promises made,
Time stands still, our fears allayed.
Your laughter dances in the air,
Symphonies of moments, shared with care.

Every sigh, a secret told,
In soft embraces, love unfolds.
Fingers interlaced, we find,
In this union, hearts aligned.

Through stormy nights and skies so clear,
We journey on, devoid of fear.
With every heartbeat, we ignite,
A love like stars that shine so bright.

As days unfold, with every glance,
In rhythm's pulse, there lies a chance.
Together we breathe, dreams unfurl,
Two heartbeats in sync, a wondrous whirl.

Gentle Flames

Dancing shadows on the wall,
Softly flicker, night's enthrall.
Whispers sing in ember's glow,
Hearts alight in warmth's flow.

Each spark a memory that glows,
Tender moments as time flows.
Feel the heat of love's embrace,
In the quiet, find our place.

Crisp air wrapped in night's embrace,
Safety found in shared space.
Together forged in soft delight,
Gentle flames guide us tonight.

Stories shared around the fire,
Kindled dreams that lift us higher.
From the past, our hopes ignite,
In the warmth of this sweet night.

With every flicker, vows we make,
In the glow, no hearts can break.
Gentle flames, our love's refrain,
Together dancing through the rain.

Melodies of Shared Laughter

In the air, our laughter rings,
Joyful notes that life now brings.
Every chuckle, a sweet song,
Binding us, where we belong.

Moments rich with silly grace,
Together in this lively space.
Whispers turn to fits of cheer,
Melodies that draw us near.

Sunlight dances on our faces,
In the warmth, time never races.
Echoes of our playful jest,
Memories we'll hold the best.

Through the tears and bright delight,
Side by side, we face the night.
Melodies that lift our souls,
In our hearts, love gently rolls.

Each shared glance, a chord we struck,
In this tune, we find our luck.
Embrace the joys life scattered,
In laughter's song, we're always gathered.

Our Secret Symphony

Beneath the stars, a whisper plays,
Creating magic in the haze.
Each heartbeat, a subtle rhyme,
In the silence, we find time.

Harmonies of dreams we share,
Softly woven, rare and fair.
Notes of love sweetly blend,
In our symphony, we transcend.

With every glance, a story told,
In a world that feels so bold.
Together, we compose our tune,
Underneath the silver moon.

Chords of joy and sorrow met,
In each note, our paths are set.
A melody that holds us tight,
Guiding through the dark of night.

Let the music softly swell,
In our hearts, where dreams still dwell.
Our secret symphony will play,
As we dance the night away.

Boundless Embrace

In your arms, the world stands still,
Every moment, time we fill.
Wrapped within a warm cocoon,
Lost in dreams, we'll touch the moon.

Every sigh, a gentle breeze,
Whispers shared with such great ease.
Fingers entwined, hope in sight,
Boundless love, our guiding light.

Through the storms, we carve our way,
In the night, we find our play.
With each heartbeat, echoes ring,
In your gaze, the joy you bring.

Softly spoken, words sincere,
In your presence, I hold dear.
Boundless skies above us gleam,
In your arms, we share a dream.

Together, woven, never apart,
Two souls dancing, one true heart.
In this embrace, we'll always stay,
Boundless love, come what may.

Illuminated Spaces

In quiet corners, light will spill,
Painting shadows against the will.
Whispers of hope, soft as glow,
In the heart's rhythm, they ebb and flow.

Through misty paths, our dreams align,
Every step taken, a sign divine.
Among the stars, our spirits twine,
Illuminated spaces, your hand in mine.

With every flicker, fears dissipate,
Creating beauty where love can wait.
In the glow of kindness, our doubts retreat,
A tapestry woven, our souls meet.

Beneath the surface, treasures lie,
Where laughter dances and spirits fly.
Together we navigate, never shy,
In illuminated spaces, you and I.

The Dance of Trust

In every glance, a silent pact,
Two souls entwined, a comforting act.
Each whisper shared, a promise made,
A rhythm born of light and shade.

With every beat, our hearts engage,
In this intricate, timeless stage.
Step by step, we learn the way,
The dance of trust, come what may.

Through laughter's spark and sorrow's fall,
We lift each other, we stand tall.
In the embrace of knowing eyes,
We find our truth, we claim the skies.

In tender moments, our spirits dance,
Embracing fate, seizing chance.
With every move, we break the mold,
The dance of trust, a story told.

Love in the Details

A fleeting glance, a gentle touch,
In tiny moments, we find so much.
The warmth of hands, a subtle sigh,
Love whispers softly, never shy.

A coffee shared on rainy days,
The way you smile, it always stays.
In laughter's echo, in silence too,
Love blooms in details, ever true.

Through tangled paths and busy hours,
We find connection, we nurture flowers.
In everyday life, sweet notes we write,
Love in the details, pure and bright.

With every memory, we build a shrine,
In sacred spaces, your heart meets mine.
Through simple joys, our lives entwine,
In the love we share, forever shine.

Embracing Our Shadows

In every corner lies a shade,
A part of us, often afraid.
But in acceptance, we find our grace,
Embracing shadows, we fill the space.

For every fear, a strength resides,
Together we stand, where love abides.
Through darkest nights, we shine so bright,
In union's warmth, we find the light.

With open hearts and tender hands,
We face the storms, together we stand.
In the mirror's gaze, we see it clear,
Embracing shadows, we shed the fear.

From pain to joy, we weave our tale,
In every struggle, we will prevail.
United in spirit, our bond will show,
Love's strength in shadows, watch it grow.

Whispers in the Quiet

In shadows deep, where silence plays,
The heartache hums in hidden ways.
Soft sighs weave through the midnight air,
Whispers of dreams, a tender despair.

Faint glimmers dance on darkened streams,
Carried along by forgotten dreams.
Whispers linger, secrets unfold,
Tales of the brave and stories untold.

Each breath contains a fleeting song,
In the quiet, we find where we belong.
With every hush, the world draws near,
Whispers entangled in hope and fear.

Glimpses of truth in silence reside,
In the stillness, our feelings confide.
Echoes around, soft as a sigh,
In whispers, the heart learns to fly.

So listen close to the air's gentle woeful,
Embrace the calm, let your spirit be hopeful.
In quiet moments, life's beauty is found,
In whispers of love that forever surround.

The Ties That Bind

Threads woven strong through laughter and tears,
In times of joy, in times of fears.
Connections formed in silence and strife,
The ties that bind through the chaos of life.

Shared glances spark an unspoken truth,
In every heart lies the wisdom of youth.
Through trials faced hand in hand,
Together we rise, together we stand.

In the tapestry woven with care,
Each knot a memory, each fiber a prayer.
With colors of hope, love paints the scene,
In the fabric of friendship, we find what it means.

The bonds we cherish, steadfast and true,
Are threads of connection that pull us through.
In moments of darkness, they shine ever bright,
The ties that bind us, our guiding light.

So hold tight the ones who share your flight,
In the journey of life, let love be your light.
For the ties that bind, in laughter or pain,
Are the treasures we keep, time's sweetest gain.

Echoes of Understanding

In the stillness, voices softly blend,
Echoes of thoughts we yearn to send.
Each whisper carries a weighty grace,
Connections forged in time and space.

Through rocky paths and winding roads,
Each story shared lightens the loads.
With every word, we start to see,
In echoes of understanding, we set each other free.

Strokes of clarity through the cluttered mind,
Building bridges as we search and find.
In the chorus of hearts, our truths align,
Echoes of love in every sign.

As we listen, we grow and learn,
In the dance of thoughts, the candles burn.
With open ears, we embrace the night,
Echoes of understanding, bringing light.

So let us cherish this sacred space,
Where echoes guide and hearts embrace.
In the symphony of souls, we find a song,
In whispers of understanding, we all belong.

Beneath the Surface

In waters deep, where shadows dwell,
Life whispers softly, a secret to tell.
The currents pulse with stories untold,
Beneath the surface, dreams unfold.

A shimmering veil hides the restless tides,
Underneath it all, where mystery resides.
Echoes of life pulse through the blue,
Beneath the surface, hidden truths brew.

In silken waves, the whispers roam,
Calling the lost to find their home.
Beneath the calm, a world thrives unseen,
In the depth of the sea, we glimpse what has been.

With every splash, a new tale begins,
The journey of life, where each soul spins.
Beneath the surface, we rise and dive,
In the dance of the tides, we truly thrive.

So dive deep into the ocean's song,
For beneath the surface is where we belong.
In the depths of connection, our spirits unite,
Beneath the surface, we find our light.

Bridging Distances

Across the seas we share our dreams,
Where whispers weave through moonlit beams.
A bond that stretches far and wide,
Together still, with hearts as guide.

Through storms that test our fragile ties,
Our laughter dances in the skies.
In every letter, every call,
We find a way to build a wall.

The miles dissolve with every sigh,
Unseen threads that bind you and I.
With every sunrise, hope shines bright,
Drawing us close, a guiding light.

In dreams we meet, no paths too great,
Hand in hand, we navigate fate.
Through time and space, our spirits blend,
Bridging distances, hearts that mend.

Though roads are long and trials seem,
Together we can chase the dream.
For love's a bridge, unyielding, strong,
In every beat, we both belong.

Kaleidoscope of Our Moments

In flickered hues, our memories spin,
A dance of colors, where dreams begin.
Through moments bright, like shards of light,
We paint the world in pure delight.

Each laugh and tear, a vibrant thread,
Woven tightly, where love is fed.
A tapestry of joy and strife,
The kaleidoscope of our shared life.

With every glance, a spark ignites,
Reflections grand in starry nights.
We chase the sun, we catch the rain,
In every heartache, love remains.

Through whispered tales and silent fears,
We treasure time, embrace the years.
A canvas filled with dreams unspun,
In every shade, we both are one.

So here we stand, two souls entwined,
In moments fleeting, love defined.
A vibrant world, forever bright,
In our kaleidoscope, pure delight.

The Warmth of Our Silence

In quietude, our hearts converse,
A language soft, a gentle verse.
No need for words, we understand,
As silence wraps us, hand in hand.

In stillness, time begins to fade,
Each heartbeat shared, a soft cascade.
We breathe together, lost in thought,
In this embrace, all else is caught.

The world outside may roar and crash,
But in this space, we make a splash.
With every glance, our souls ignite,
In warmth of silence, pure and bright.

We find our peace in sacred hush,
No rush to speak, no need to rush.
Each moment lingers, rich and sweet,
In quietude, our hearts compete.

So let us linger in this calm,
A gentle balm, a soothing psalm.
For in the quiet, love transcends,
The warmth of silence, never ends.

Fragments of Forever

In shattered glass, we find the light,
Each piece reflects a love so bright.
With every crack, a story spun,
Fragments of forever, two become one.

Through storms we weather, side by side,
In every challenge, we take pride.
The scars we bear, they tell our tale,
A testament that will not pale.

We gather moments like scattered stars,
In every heartbeat, no more bars.
The universe, a canvas vast,
With fragments of forever, love is cast.

In laughter's echo and sorrow's sigh,
Together we rise, we learn to fly.
For every piece that breaks apart,
Is just a way to shape the heart.

So here's to us, imperfectly whole,
Embracing every flawed little role.
In every fragment, we boldly soar,
For love is timeless—fragments of forevermore.

The Pulse of Connection

In the quiet of the night, we find,
Threads of laughter, joy intertwined.
Hearts beating softly, a rhythm so sweet,
In every heartbeat, our souls meet.

Under the stars, we share hopes anew,
Words spoken softly, promises too.
With each embrace, a story unfolds,
Capturing moments, more precious than gold.

Together we wander, through valleys and peaks,
In silence we listen, and time gently speaks.
Whispers of friendship, nurtured with care,
In the pulse of connection, we're always aware.

Every glance shared paints the canvas bright,
Through shadows and light, we foster the light.
Hand in hand, we journey, a tapestry spun,
In the rhythm of life, we are never done.

Illuminating Our Journey

With each step forward, the path reveals,
A dance of shadows, a canvas that feels.
Guided by stars, our dreams softly gleam,
In the night's embrace, we begin to dream.

Every turn taken, a lesson well learned,
In the flickers of hope, our spirits are turned.
Together we traverse through darkness and light,
Illuminating the journey, igniting the night.

The whispers of trees tell tales from the past,
Reminding us gently, our moments will last.
In harmony's song, we find our own way,
Through valleys of shadows and bright fields of day.

Footprints in sand mark the days that we've shared,
Each moment a treasure, with love we've declared.
Illuminating paths where our hearts come alive,
With every breath taken, we learn to thrive.

So let us wander, hand in hand, brave,
With courage and hope, our dreams we will save.
On this journey of ours, let the heart be the guide,
Illuminating our journey, forever beside.

Weaving Together Time

In the loom of existence, threads intertwine,
Each moment a pattern, both complex and fine.
Time dances gently, with colors so bright,
Weaving together, day into night.

With laughter like silk, and tears like the rain,
We stitch our tomorrows, through joy and through pain.
In the tapestry's heart lies the stories we tell,
Each woven together, casting a spell.

Echoes of moments, both near and afar,
A quilt of our lives, under the same star.
Today and tomorrow, in harmony rhyme,
Together we create, weaving together time.

As seasons change, so too do our dreams,
Yet in every thread, familiar it seems.
With threads of compassion, we fortify bonds,
Building a legacy that forever responds.

So let us embrace every twist, every turn,
In the fabric of life, there's so much to learn.
Weaving together the essence of life,
A communal journey, flavored with strife.

Moments of Clarity

In the still of the dawn, clarity speaks,
A whisper of wisdom, the heart gently seeks.
In fleeting seconds, truth comes to light,
Revealing the shadows that dance out of sight.

Each breath we take, an echo of grace,
Moments of clarity shape time and space.
In the chaos of life, a stillness we find,
Inviting reflection, uniting the mind.

Through laughter and tears, we're learning to see,
The beauty in struggle, the power to be.
In those quiet breaths where the world fades away,
Moments of clarity guide us each day.

When storms rage above and clouds loom so near,
In the heart's gentle whisper, we conquer our fear.
For in every heartbeat, the truth softly sways,
Moments of clarity, our guiding rays.

So let us embrace each lesson with grace,
Finding clarity's light in the vastness of space.
For in the journey we share, we uncover the way,
Moments of clarity, our compass each day.

A Beacon in the Dark

In the shadows, light shall gleam,
A flicker bursts, ignites the dream.
Hope ascends on fragile wings,
Guiding souls to brighter things.

A lighthouse standing firm and true,
Its guiding rays breaking through.
In stormy seas, it calls our name,
A steadfast fire, an endless flame.

Night may cloak the hidden path,
Yet every heart can brave the wrath.
With every step, we'll feel the spark,
Together we can face the dark.

So hold the light within your heart,
For darkness fades, we'll never part.
With each dawn, a chance to start,
A beacon lives within us, part.

And when the world seems cold and bleak,
Look for the hope, for that you seek.
In unity, we stand apart,
Forever guided by love's art.

Layers of You and Me

Beneath the skin, a world resides,
A story told where silence hides.
With every touch, we peel away,
To find the truth in shades of grey.

In whispered dreams, our layers blend,
With every twist, a chance to mend.
Fragments of laughter, tears we share,
In this tapestry, we lay bare.

Colors of past meet hues of now,
In every moment, we take a vow.
To cherish what the heart unveils,
In love's embrace where hope prevails.

You bring the dawn, I hold the night,
Together we create our light.
With every heartbeat, we entwine,
Layer on layer, love's design.

So let us dive into the deep,
In pools of dreams where secrets sleep.
The layers may be thick or thin,
But love's our guide, we'll always win.

The Depths We Dive

Beneath the waves, in silence deep,
Where dreams and shadows softly creep.
We plunge into the unknown blue,
With courage fierce and hearts so true.

The water's chill wraps us tight,
Yet in the depths, we find our light.
With every stroke, we journey far,
In endless seas, we chase the star.

Coral gardens, treasures rare,
In every moment, we find care.
With ebb and flow, we learn to be,
In the great dance of you and me.

So let the currents pull us near,
In whispered waves, we shed our fear.
With every breath, we redefine,
The depths of love, eternally mine.

Together we emerge anew,
From fathoms deep, with skies so blue.
With memories forged in ocean's tide,
Embracing wide, the depths we dive.

Whispers in the Silence

In quiet spaces, secrets bloom,
Where shadows dance and thoughts consume.
Amidst the hush, a voice will rise,
In tender sighs, love never lies.

The wind carries your name so sweet,
In stillness, every heartbeat meet.
Like echoes of a distant song,
In silence, we have always belonged.

Through veils of time, we slowly weave,
In whispered words, we dare believe.
For in the hush, emotions flow,
A hidden garden set to grow.

When chaos reigns and noise prevails,
We find our strength through muted trails.
With every breath, a soft refrain,
In silent love, we break the chain.

So let us linger in the calm,
In tranquil moments, find the balm.
For whispers linger in the night,
In silent love, our spirits light.

Illuminated Pathways

Beneath the stars, we walk so free,
Paths aglow, like dreams to be.
With every step, the shadows fade,
In light we trust, our fears unmade.

Whispers lingering in the night,
Guiding us with soft, warm light.
Hands entwined, we share our tales,
Through ups and downs, our love prevails.

The moon above, a guiding star,
Reminds us just how close we are.
In the quiet, hearts align,
On this journey, you are mine.

Moments cherished, lost in time,
In this dance, a perfect rhyme.
With every breath, a promise made,
On illuminated pathways laid.

Together we'll face what's to come,
In joyful hearts, we find our home.
Through every night, through every day,
We walk this path, come what may.

Mosaic of Memories

Fragments of laughter, snippets of song,
In the heart's gallery, we all belong.
Colors so vivid, tales intertwined,
In a mosaic of memories, love defined.

Each piece tells a story, a moment so dear,
Echoes of friendship that we hold near.
Whispers of seasons that come and go,
In the tapestry woven, our spirits glow.

From golden summers to winter's chill,
We gather each memory, our hearts to fill.
The bonds that we forge, through laughter and tears,
Create a mosaic that spans through the years.

In each little shard, a life intertwined,
In the canvas of time, harmony we find.
With colors that shift, yet still they unite,
In this mosaic of memories, pure delight.

As we walk through the gallery, hand in hand,
We embrace every moment, together we stand.
In each little piece, we find our way home,
In this endless journey, we're never alone.

A Symphony of Souls

In the silence, music starts to play,
A symphony of souls in a graceful array.
Each note a story, each chord a dream,
Together we rise like a flowing stream.

In harmonious whispers, our spirits align,
The rhythm of life, in perfect design.
With every heartbeat, the echoes blend,
In this beautiful journey, there's no end.

From melodies soft to crescendos bold,
Our voices unite, a tale to be told.
With laughter and love, we create our song,
In the symphony of souls, where we all belong.

When the world is quiet, we softly sing,
In the dance of life, together we bring.
Every note carries the warmth of embrace,
A symphony resounding, our sacred space.

Through highs and lows, we find our way,
In the orchestra of dreams, we sway.
With each passing moment, the music plays on,
In this symphony of souls, we are never withdrawn.

The Rhythm of Togetherness

In the heartbeat of morning, we rise anew,
Together we shine, in all that we do.
With every sunrise, a promise to keep,
The rhythm of togetherness runs deep.

Side by side through laughter, side by side through tears,
We conquer our doubts, embrace our fears.
With melodies sung on the journey we make,
In the rhythm of togetherness, love will awake.

With hands intertwined, we dance through the night,
Creating our steps, in the soft moonlight.
Each pulse a reminder, of where we belong,
In the rhythm of togetherness, we are strong.

Through every season, as changes unfold,
Our bond is the treasure, more precious than gold.
In joy and in sorrow, together we sway,
The rhythm of togetherness, guiding our way.

As time moves along, may we always find,
The beauty in moments, the grace intertwined.
With hearts in sync, we'll continue to grow,
In the rhythm of togetherness, forever we'll flow.

Embracing Our Shadows

In the quiet hour of night,
We find the whispers of the past.
Shadows dance beneath the light,
In their embrace, we are cast.

Fear not the darkness which lies near,
It teaches lessons we must learn.
Embrace the flaws, the hidden fear,
For in the shadows, hearts discern.

We gather strength from what we hide,
A tapestry of light and dark.
Through the pain, the soul has cried,
We light the path, ignite the spark.

The silhouette of who we are,
Reflects the beauty of our plight.
In shadow's fold, we find the star,
A beacon shining through the night.

Together we can face the truth,
No longer bound by fear or pride.
For every scar reveals our youth,
In shadows, love and hope reside.

The Gentle Rub of Truth

Like soft hands brushing on the skin,
Truth reveals itself in time.
With tender care, it seeks within,
Peeling layers, rough and prime.

Each revelation, a gentle sigh,
Echoes in the heart so deep.
It lifts the soul up to the sky,
Awakens dreams that dare to leap.

In honesty, we find our place,
A warmth that holds, a tender grip.
Through every tear, a healing grace,
The truth is like a steady ship.

As we navigate the tides of night,
The gentle rub guides us through.
With every star that shines so bright,
We learn the steps to start anew.

So let us trust the journey's flow,
For truth, though soft, is strong and clear.
With every pulse, an inner glow,
Together facing what we fear.

Through the Eyes of Trust

In the stillness, we align,
With every heartbeat, feel the rise.
Through the eyes of trust, we shine,
Awakening the world, surprise.

Each glance a promise, soft and true,
Reflecting bonds that never break.
In every moment, me and you,
Together standing, we won't shake.

Through trials faced, we lift the veil,
Unfurling layers love has sewn.
With trust as our enduring trail,
We chart the course, we seek the known.

With open hearts and gentle ways,
We weave our stories, side by side.
In trust, we find the light of days,
Where shadows fade and love abides.

Let every whisper guide our path,
Through tangled roots and branching trees.
In every laughter, feel the math,
Of trust that sways in every breeze.

Navigating the Depths

In oceans vast where currents sway,
We voyage into the unknown.
With courage, hearts will find a way,
Through depths where seeds of truth are sown.

The water's pulse, a rhythm strong,
Guides us through tempests and calm.
In every tide, we all belong,
Facing our fears, we become the balm.

With every wave that sweeps our feet,
We gather strength from rise and fall.
Embracing fears that we must meet,
To stand together through it all.

We delve into the mysteries deep,
Where shadows hide and whispers play.
For only then can we truly leap,
And find our light in every gray.

Through depths we learn, we grow, we trust,
In waters dark, the jewels gleam.
Navigating paths is quite a must,
In every challenge lies the dream.

9 789916 890677